Buying Or Selling A Small Business

What You Need To Know Before You Buy Or Sell

Steven Imke

Produced in the United States of America

First Printing, 2016

ISBN-13: 978-1534699540
ISBN-10: 1534699546

KSI Enterprises
395 Scrub Oak Circle
Monument CO 80132

www.SteveBizBlog.com

About the Author

Steve's first foray into the world of small business came when he was an Invisible Fencing dealer. He operated this business on a part-time basis while remaining employed by a Fortune 500 company called Digital Equipment Corporation (DEC). While the Invisible Fencing business was not very successful for Steve, it was a valuable opportunity for him to learn important lessons about business in a relatively low-risk environment.

After ending his relationship with Invisible Fencing, he worked on a business plan for a new business idea and waited for the right opportunity to present itself. In 1994, DEC fell on hard times. Instead of bemoaning this turbulent economic tide, Steve capitalized on this opportunity. He quit his day job at DEC to found Horizon Interactive, a documentation and training company. In fact, Horizon Interactive became a vendor for DEC.

Over the next few years, Steve and his partners executed the business plan. The business grew to over $3 million in annual sales and opened offices in several states. Horizon Interactive's success drew the attention of Interleaf, a publicly held company out of Massachusetts. In 1999, Interleaf acquired Horizon Interactive.

As part of the acquisition, Steve was offered the position of VP of Operations for their services division. Under his leadership, Interleaf acquired two more businesses like

Horizon Interactive. The company grew the services side of the business from a combined $8 million in revenue to over $32 million in sales during the next two years.

In 2001, Interleaf was acquired by Broadvision, a California company during the height of the dot com era. Broadvision primarily acquired Interleaf for their XML engineers who worked on the product side of the business. Needing to divest himself from the services business, Steve and a former business partner acquired the assets of Interleaf's service business and started IC Interactive. They operated the business for a few more years until they sold it in 2003.

Being a serial entrepreneur, Steve has started and still operates three different businesses. One of his businesses is focused on real estate. The second one is focused on oil and gas. His third business is a company designed to help high net-worth investors understand the ins and outs of investing in oil and gas direct participation programs.

Steve has volunteered his time since 2003 as a mentor for SCORE, a local organization dedicated to helping entrepreneurs. He has acted as their Chapter Chairman for several years. He is also an advisory board member of his local Small Business Development Center (SBDC). In additions to his advisory role, he also acts as a counselor for the SBDC since 2003. In 2012, Steve acted as the interim director of SBDC while they conducted a national search for a permanent director. Currently, Steve is the Entrepreneurship Director at Pikes Peak Community College and writes a daily blog about small businesses.

Steve is a flaming dyslexic, which has its good points and bad points. Growing up, he remembers undergoing a board of education evaluation. When asked to draw a tree, Steve drew a series of concentric rings. When asked about his drawing, he said the rings were what you see when you cut down the tree and look at the stump. These rings tell the entire life story of the tree. The evaluator told his parents he was not normal. He should be more like the other kids and draw the tree from the side view.

However, rather than conform to the crowd, Steve embraced his out-of-the-box thinking as an asset. The upside of being dyslexic is exceptional spatial awareness and problems solving skills. Dyslexics develop these heightened skills since they are forced from an early age to compensate for things they do not do well.

Being a dyslexic in school prevented Steve from becoming a good reader. Even today, spelling and grammar are not his strong suits. Academically, Steve struggled in traditional schools. When he graduated from high school, he knew that a traditional classroom education was not for him so he joined the United States Coast Guard to learn a trade. Graduating near the top of his class in tech school, Steve realized that he learned by doing.

Steve tends to be an overly logical person. He likes to explore, document, and measure nearly every aspect of a project to find out what works and what does not. He has a propensity to focus on understanding why things are the way they are rather than how to duplicate what others have already done. Once Steve obtains a reasonable level of mastery in a specific subject area, he internalizes the knowledge and moves on to his next area of interest.

Everything of substance Steve knows about small business initially began by him reading books, listening to audiobooks, or watching others. He internalizes the salient points, then rolls up his sleeves and puts them into practice in his own business. Once Steve perfects a lesson, he makes it a point to document it and then share it with others. He calls these "Sea Stories," leveraging his old Coast Guard days. In addition to sharing his knowledge, this practice serves to further solidify his learning in his own mind while continuing to grow his knowledge base. In this way, Steve has codified over more than a decade's worth of his small business knowledge in the various books he has written.

This process has served Steve pretty well. By the time he was 42 years old, Steve had reached the point where he no longer needed to work for money. Passing this income milestone has not only allowed him the luxury to spend even more time to ponder and digest life's lessons, but also the freedom to tell it like it is without the fear of losing his job. He proudly wears jeans nearly every day. He also sports facial hair to remind himself and others that being a nonconformist and not subscribing to traditional viewpoints has its merits for entrepreneurs.

Steve constantly reads and listens to non-fiction audiobooks about politics or business related topics. He consumes current events from a huge basket of news sources every day so he can relate their messages in new and innovative ways. After internalizing a message and testing new theories, he shares his new-found wisdom with people willing to listen.

Since 2003, Steve has mentored and counseled thousands of fledgling entrepreneurs through his volunteer efforts with SCORE and SBDC. He has volunteered his expertise to help organizations like ARC, a program which helps individuals with developmental disabilities.

As cliché as it may sound, Steve is at the point in his life where it is all about using his skills and knowledge to help others to succeed. Steve never expects anything in return, but simply enjoys the appreciation he receives from the people he has helped and lives vicariously through their success. For Steve, sharing his knowledge is akin to the feeling a billionaire might have handing out $100 bills to random strangers on the street. He knows that by sharing some of the wisdom he has accumulated with clients, he can often make a positive difference in their lives. Steve is not particularly religious so helping entrepreneurs is his way of giving back and making a significant impact on the world around him.

Table of Contents

Chapter 1: Overview

3 Risk Levels to Becoming a Business Owner

Most of the clients I see want to start their business from scratch, but there are 2 other options to becoming a business owner.

The first option is to buy an existing business and the second is to buy a franchise. Clients often tell me that these two options simply cost too much. They argue that they are choosing to start from scratch because it is the cheaper path.

At that point in the conversation, I often remind them that starting a business from scratch is by far the riskiest way to become a business owner. In fact, statistics from the US Department of Commerce say that;

65% to 90% of start-up business are likely to fail within the first five years. In other words, only 10% to 35% will have a chance of success.

The principle reason for this high failure rate is that most businesses take on too many fixed expenses early on. On top of that, their revenue ramps up slower than planned and the business simply runs out of money before breaking even and turning a profit.

One client who had previously been a pilot in the US Air Force summed it up best when he said;

"I guess they had too much payload and not enough runway."

Entrepreneurs that buy an existing business have a 90% to 95% chance of still being in business after 5 years.

The principle reason for this higher success rate is that when you buy an existing business, you already have revenue from customers and have a predictable level of expenses. You know these expenses are less than the amount of revenue, which leaves the business some profit and cash flow to work with.

Moreover, existing businesses often have employees that already know their jobs, are well trained, and the business has proven processes to capture customer value.

Entrepreneurs that buy into a franchise concept have a 90% chance of still being in business after 5 years.

Although franchises need new customers to generate revenue, the entrepreneur is often buying brand awareness and a proven system.

Moreover, most new franchises are able to reduce the cost of goods sold by taking advantage of the economies of scale established by the franchiser since they have franchise-wide buying power.

When you buy a franchise or another person's business, you also have access to someone who knows both the business and financial model as well as someone who has a vested interest in your success. Obviously this is not the case with start-ups. Let's not forget that the primary goal of business ownership is to make money for the owner.

Existing businesses make money on day one. A successful franchise will earn the owner income not too long after starting up. However, a start-up, even one that survives, may take months or even years to begin to pay the owner a salary for working in the business.

When it comes to business ownership, have you considered buying vs. starting from scratch?

Why Owners Sell Their Business

I teach a boot camp class each month for our local Small Business Development Center (SBDC). There is portion of this course that looks at the three ways to become a business owner. These ways as stated above include: buying a business, buying a franchise, and starting from scratch.

As I discuss the option of buying an existing business, I often hear someone in the audience say, "Aren't you just buying someone else's failing business when you buy an existing business?" While some owners may be trying to pawn off their failing business, these businesses can be weeded out with proper due diligence. The number one reason owners sell their business is boredom or burnout.

To counter the notion that all businesses for sale are dogs, I'd like to share a few of the most popular reasons business owners elect to sell their business.

Lack of Operating/Growth Capital
Lack of operating or growth capital is a very common reason the founder chooses to sell a product-based or lifestyle business.

If you ever watch ABC's Shark Tank, you will see many great ideas that can't seem to break through due to a lack of risk capital on the part of the founder. Sometimes they have invested all of their savings to get a working prototype and no longer have the means or marketing expertise to get the company going. For the product to reach the light of day, the business needs fresh ideas and fresh capital.

Sometimes start-up founders realize their shortcomings and may simply be looking to add a partner or investor with complementary business skills and talents. Remember, most companies have more than a single owner so you don't have to be the founder or sole owner to be a business owner.

Borrowing Capacity

When it comes to debt financing, the small business owner is almost always the guarantor of any loan. The financial obligation to the company as a guarantor of a loan can often impact a person's personal borrowing capacity such as when they are buying a new home or car.

Moreover, being a personal guarantor on business loans can be a heavy burden for many people. They can reach a threshold and decide to sell a business to eliminate their personal guarantees.

Age

Of course age can be a factor, especially if the business requires a high degree of physical labor. Many years ago we had a custom hot tub designed and built by a local hot tub company. We continued to use the services of this company from time to time to fix leaks and replace failing parts. One day the owner said to me that he was going to sell the business because his body just could not take the rigors of working in the freezing cold. He also could no longer crawl into tight places under and around the tubs to repair leaks without experiencing pain which leads to the next reason owners sell.

Health
Similar to age, another reason for selling a business is that the owner or a close family member may be experiencing health-related issues. Running the business is just too big a demand on their time if a close family member is dealing with a long-term illness like cancer.

Economic Diversity
Business owners are often all financially in when it comes to their business. As the economy undulates, it favors different industries. Without a degree of income diversification, dips in economic cycles can spell doom for some owners. They do not have other sources of income to weather bad economic spells. Therefore, some owners will start a business and then cash out. Smart business owners will use the funds to perhaps start another endeavor, but hold back some in reserve for a rainy day. They may even invest in other businesses or industries to achieve a level of diversification.

For example, I had a residential real estate development business in the early to mid 2000's The housing boom was in full swing and I was making good money. However it was concentrating too much of my net worth in one industry, residential real estate. I sold several of my model homes and rolled over the profits into a few key commercial income properties with long term leases. I then used the reserves to start an oil and gas business to achieve a level of income diversification. Oil prices soared to $120 per barrel while the income from the commercial property business remained relatively flat during the housing bubble collapse. The income diversity providing me the ability to weather the 2008 financial crisis that would have been disastrous for me had I stayed concentrated in residential real estate.

Fund Buy Out
The last reason why business owners elect to sell their business is to fund a buy out. Sometimes a partner dies or gets divorced and the owner needs to sell the business to fund a settlement.

Go to this book's video supplement page at www.stevebizblog.com/buysell-videos to see a video of Ron Chernak and John Zayac two owners of M&A brokerage houses, explaining why their clients decided to sell their businesses.

Do you know the real reason the business owner is selling his business?

Why Buyers Buy a Business

The inverse to why sellers sell a business is why buyers buy. Often a seller may only sell one business in a lifetime. However, buyers often buy several companies during their lifetime as they assemble pieces to help another business grow. Many buyers purchase a business to avoid the risk associated with start-ups and are principally financial buyers. However, many times the buyer is a strategic buyer who is looking for a business to shore up a need in another business.

For example, I purchased the assets of a complementary documentation business in Milwaukee, WI to diversify my client base and expand my geography. My client base was too heavily concentrated in the computer and tel-co sectors. In fact, my client base was dominated by only two very large companies. The acquisition allowed me to diversify my overall concentration, making my bankers happy and my business much more attractive to potential buyers.

Often buyers buy a business because they see growth potential that the seller does not see or does not have access to. Other times the buyer is looking for a strategic fit or to create line extensions. For example, DuraLog had a nice business selling fireplace logs during the winter, but sales in the summer were nonexistent. Kingsford had a nice business selling charcoal briquettes during the summer, but winters were a brutal time for them. The merger of

DuraLog and Kingsford allowed each to fix its seasonal fluctuations.

Sometimes, the buyer is looking to increase utilization of its fixed assets such as a manufacturing plant that has extra capacity.

Many times, the buyer is buying assets that don't appear on a balance sheet. For instance, these assets might include the seller's customer base, vendor base, employees, patents, or industry knowledge. After my business was acquired, I stayed on to help them build up and grow their business until it too was acquired by another company. The reason for the acquisition was that the company that originally acquired me employed half of all the XML engineers on the planet at the time and the company just wanted the XML engineers.

Why would potential buyers look at buying your business?

Types of Business Buyers

When it comes to the buyer of a business, buyers fall into one of two basic categories: financial buyers and strategic buyers.

Financial Buyers

Financial buyers value a business based on its past earnings, but decide to buy a particular business based upon its future earning potential. While small lifestyle businesses are often bought by individuals, larger businesses are primarily bought by investment groups and high net worth investors.

Strategic Buyers

Strategic buyers, also called synergistic buyers, may value a business based on its past earnings, but decide to buy a business based on its intangible assets. Often strategic buyers are buying things you never anticipated.

In one case, I recall a struggling lumber yard was bought on the cheap. The sell just assumed that it was going to sell its business to a financial buyer. Because its sales were declining they thought that the business could not command a premium price. In reality, the buyer was a strategic buyer who had no intention of operating the lumber yard after the purchase. The strategic buyer was actually purchasing a deep water dock on the property of lumber yard.

Strategic buyers are often competitors who want your intangible assets, market share, or location. They could even be customers that want to expand their business downstream or vendors looking to expand upstream.

Go to this book's video supplement page at www.stevebizblog.com/buysell-videos to see a video of what the experts have to say about who are the buyers of small business.

Can you tell the difference between a financial and strategic buyer?

Types of Business Purchases

Basically, businesses are purchased either as an asset purchase or a stock purchase. That said, most sales of small businesses are treated as an asset sale. In fact, if the business being sold is a sole proprietorship, a partnership, or a LLC that doesn't issue stock, the transaction is an always going to be an asset sale. While the sale of a corporation can also be treated as an asset sale, it can be structured as a stock sale.

As a buyer, you generally want to buy assets. However, as a seller, you may want to sell stock for better tax treatment. As a buyer, when you buy assets vs. stock, you leave behind any potential hidden liabilities. Consequently, it is less risky for the buyer to buy a business as an asset purchase. Moreover, as the buyer, you will want to allocate most of the sale to tangible items that are not depreciated over time. You will want to write up and allocate most of the sales price to intangibles such as goodwill, non-compete, and consulting agreements.

Stock sales are available to corporations and if available, they are generally preferred by the seller. This is especially true if the entity is a c-corp so the seller avoids the potential of double taxation. Moreover, it eliminates the risk to the seller if there are hidden liabilities.

Go to this books video supplement page at www.stevebizblog.com/buysell-videos to see a video of

Chris Blees, the President & CEO of a large CPA firm specializing in M&A, explaining the difference between an asset and a stock transaction.

Will you be buying or selling assets or stock in the near future?

Business Cycle Economics and Selling a Business

When the seller makes the decision to sell his business, time is often his worst enemy. Many things outside of the seller's control can often negatively effect the value of the business.

For example, changes in the industry can make elements of the business obsolete. The interest rate hikes by lenders can make your business more expensive in the long run for the buyer. The volatility of the stock market might make the buyer think twice about liquidating stock from his portfolio to come up with his down payment. Also, tax laws could change the total return of the investment and of course changes in the economy can also affect the value of the business.

Once you decide it is the right time to sell, you need to do whatever it takes to accelerate the sales process. Don't just leave it out there, hoping that one day a buyer will come along.

Are you doing everything you can to sell your business fast?

Recasting Financial Reports When Selling Your Business

When it is time for an owner to sell his business, the wise seller will "recast" his financial reports to create a clearer and often better impression of his business for the buyer to see. If you are the buyer and the seller has not recast his financial statements, you'll want to recast them yourself to get a better picture of the true value of the business.

To recast the financial reports, the seller will start with his P&L, also known as an income statement. I recommend exporting the P&L into a spreadsheet and adding three additional columns to the right. One column, label "Adjustments." Label the next column "Recasted," which is the adjusted value after accounting for the adjustment. Finally, label the third column "Note."

Actual	Adjustment	Recasted	Note
$35,584		$35,584	
$275,021		$275,021	
$26,023		$26,023	
$336,628	$0	$336,628	
$78,527	$296,473	$375,000	1
$78,527	$296,473	$375,000	

When I counsel the seller, I have them examine each discretionary expense and add an adjustment to remove any operation expense or portion of an operating expense that was for their own benefit as well as many other nonreoccuring operating expenses.

Some example of expenses that benefit the owner include:
- personal auto usage
- insurance
- travel
- cell phone charges
- and other expenses that are clearly for the benefit of the owner and not necessary for business operations.

Additionally, the seller will add adjustments to remove any depreciation, amortization, and interest since after the sale these will change.

Moreover, all P&L line items need to be normalized to adjust for nonreoccurring income and expenses.

Go to this book's video supplement page at www.stevebizblog.com/buysell-videos to see a video from three M&A experts explaining recastable items.

For example, I once had a major project that was canceled unexpectedly. Rather than lay off the employees involved when the funding stopped, I kept them for way too long in the hopes of getting them new work. When none materialized, I then gave them a generous severance package. When I recast my financial reports, I adjusted out the salaries of the affected employees as well as the cost of the severance package since a new owner may have handled the situation differently.

In addition, the owner's salary is also backed out as well since the new owner will choose his own salary.

For each of the adjustments, I add a note number in the last column and provide a description for each adjustment at the end of the document that corresponds to the footnote number.

Do you recast your financial reports to determine a clearer picture of a company's value?

How to Find and Evaluate a Business for Sale

Perhaps you have decided to become a business owner but starting up your own business is just too risky. One way to locate business that are for sale is to go to the online business for sale marketplace. Two popular online business marketplaces are BizBuySell.com and BizQuest.com.

Another option includes finding a local business or franchise broker by checking the classifies for business opportunities or businesses for sale.

Another way that most people often don't think about is to simply approach a business you would consider owning and ask the owner if he has ever considered selling. Even if he is not willing to sell, he may be able to refer you to someone else who is.

When you find a prospective small business with under one million dollars in revenue, remember that in all likelihood the business was run in a taxed advantaged way for the benefit of the owner. If this is the case, put more stock on the revenue than the reported taxable income initially.

Regardless of the business's size, consider next what you would do differently from the current owner. A simple rule of thumb is to base one half of the decision on what the seller did and the other half on what you would do differently.

Whenever you consider buying another person's business, you should always develop your own preliminary business plan to see what you might do differently. Some minor improvement that can pay large dividends to the buyer are as simple as staying open longer, changing prices, motivating employees, marketing more, adding a drive through, building a better marketing process or website, and adding pickup and delivery services.

Using the Business Model Canvas at this point can be an eye opening experience. A key point here is you pay the seller on his past performance, but value the business on potential future earnings.

When it comes to trying to determine the income potential, you will have to account for any debt service related to the purchase. Additionally, the seller generally takes the cash in the business and well as gets paid for the accounts receivable up to the sale date at the closing. You, as the new owner, have to inject a sufficient amount of cash into the business to cover the operating expenses until your own receivables kick in.

When it comes to lifestyle or micro businesses, remember that the financial reports alone may not paint an accurate picture of the owner's true compensation. Small business owners often use business assets for personal use. For example, a farmer may slaughter a cow for personal consumption that never shows up on the books or a fleet vehicle may be used to benefit the owner and not be accounted for on the books.

Are you ready to buy a business?

Chapter 2: Valuations

Factors that Effect Business Value

There are several factors that can positively and negatively affect the value of a business from the point of view of the buyer. Some common factors that add value to a business include:

- The organization, including its employees and internal processes
- Its reputation in the industry
- How well the business fits with the acquiring business, including the culture
- Terms of the final deal
- How "hot" the industry is and if it's getting hotter
- Overall market conditions
- Other intangibles
- Timing of the offer
- Number of competing offers

Go to this book's video supplement page at www.stevebizblog.com/buysell-videos to see a video of Ron Chernak, a business broker talking about intangible assets that add value to a business.

When I sold my first business, the payment was to be made in the acquiring company's public stock. Since it was during the dot com era, stock prices reflected the good market conditions and were on the rise. Also, the acquiring company had a hard deadline for the transaction since it needed to complete the transaction prior to its year end close. This deadline added value to my business so I began to increase my demands as the closing date got closer. Therefore, I was able to leverage several factors that enhanced the value of my business from the prospective of the buyer.

On the flip side, there are factors that can discount the value of a business from the prospective of the buyer, including:

- Employment-related liabilities
- Environmental liabilities
- Litigation liabilities
- Tax liabilities
- Product warranty liabilities
- Contract liabilities
- Duress by seller such as health or monetary issues
- Lack of time to complete the deal on the part of the seller
- Not using an intermediary to remove emotions
- Coming to an agreement too quickly/easily
- Only one offer
- Overall seller naïvety since a buyer may buy many businesses while a seller often only sells a business once

Go to this book's video supplement page at www.stevebizblog.com/buysell-videos to see a video of Ron Chernak and John Zayac two owners of large M&A brokerage houses, explaining ways to enhance or detract from a company's value.

What are the factors that can add value to your business or acquisition target? What factors subtract from its value?

How to Value an Existing Lifestyle or Micro Business

When it comes to buying a business, size does matters. Most lifestyle or micro businesses have under 1 million in annual sales. When it comes to lifestyle and micro businesses, the owner is also the top manager.

For valuation purposes, a good rule of thumb for a marketable lifestyle or micro business is that the owner should generally earn about 10 to 20% of the gross sales.

Therefore, a lifestyle or micro business that does $400k in revenue should have an owner that earns between $40k to $80k per year from owning and working in the business.

Often when the million dollar gross sales per year threshold is eclipsed, the owner's income drops to 10% or less. This drop is mostly due to the need to increase management,which leads to thinner margins, and higher inventory or carrying costs.

In summary, the important issue for you as a buyer is how much can you expect to earn?

When it comes to lifestyle and micro businesses where the owner is responsible for managing employees, taking care of customers, and other day-to-day activities, the owner likely views bookkeeping as a low priority. If anything, he relies on compiled financial reports and is far less inclined to use these reports to run their business. Therefore any financial records provided by the seller may be less accurate and require more due diligence on the part of the buyer.

From the prospective of an accountant or a banker, the value of a business is purely based on historical financial statements, which can be an incomplete view of a company's real value.

Other factors that drive the value of a business is its location, equipment, inventory, employees, patents, existing customer base, industry, vendor supplier relations, completion, and what you plan to do with the business after a sale. Therefore, you cannot rely on your accountant or banker to define a quantitative value of a business you are looking to buy.

Other value drivers aside, another rule of thumb is that businesses often sell for a little more than two times discretionary earnings.

To understand discretionary earnings, you must first understand that a small business is an economic entity that provides a product or service that customers buy in sufficient quantities to allow the owner to pay all costs and operating expenses, including the owner's salary.

Let's say that water represents revenue and a bucket

represents the volume of all non-discretionary costs and operating expenses such as rent, employ salary (including a fair wage for the owner), marketing, insurance utilities, etc.

The lip of the bucket represents the breaking even point of discretionary income. The water or revenue that overflows the bucket is considered discretionary income.

Let me be clear– discretionary income is not yet profit since the surplus revenue can be used in a variety of ways. The owner can use the surplus to buy more inventory, increase his promotional expenses, pay off debt, or pay himself more money.

It is the discretionary income that is most often used to value a business. According to a business broker's friend, with over 15-year experience selling businesses, the average selling price for lifestyle and micro business was 2.3 times the business's discretionary earnings.

Do you know how to value a lifestyle or micro business?

5 Reasons for a Business Valuation

There are many reasons to conduct a business valuation. Some valuations are pretty straight forward while others can be quite complicated. If there is a good possibility that the valuation will be challenged on legal grounds or by the IRS, it is often best to have the valuation performed by a qualified appraiser.

That said, I have counseled scores of clients on business valuation issues and I have come to the conclusion that there are five primary reasons for conducting a business valuation.

1. The first and clearly the most popular reason for conducting a business valuation is related to some form of merger & acquisition (M&A) activity. Most of the time, it is the buyer that is attempting to value the business they are considering buying.
2. Another reason to conduct a business valuation is related to estate planning. When a family owned business is passed on, there may be estate and gift taxes involved. The American Tax Relief Act of 2012 set the exclusion of estate and gift taxes at $5 million with a maximum of 40% estate tax above this threshold.
3. As new members enter and exit a closely held business, there is often a need to establish shareholder or membership values for some form of

buy/sell arrangement.

4. Intergenerational transfers of ownership often involve transferring a mix of assets to several parties. Allocating them among the parties requires an understanding of the value of the asset.

5. Finally, some owners choose to covey their ownership to their employees through an Employee Stock Ownership Program (ESOP), which requires credible evidence of the value of the business.

Do you need to perform a business valuation?

Rule of Thumb Appraisal Method

The Rule of Thumb Appraisal Method is a method often used to compute the approximate value of closely held small businesses. This method relies on a multiple of some unit of measure. The unit of measure changes based on the type of business or industry. It may be the number of subscribers, gross annual commissions, or even gross annual sales.

The following table comes from BizStats.com, which is a reliable source for Rule of Thumb valuations.

Industry	Rule of Thumb Valuation
Accounting Firms	100–125% of annual revenues
Auto Dealers (New Cars)	0–10% of annual sales + inventory
Book Stores	15% of annual sales + inventory
Coffee Shops (Gourmet)	40% of annual sales + inventory
Day Care Centers	45–50% of annual sales incl. inventory
Dental Practices	60–65% of annual revenues incl. inventory
Dry Cleaners	70–80% of annual sales + Inventory
Engineering Services	40–45% of annual revenues
Flower Shops	30–35% of annual sales + inventory
Food Shops (Gourmet)	30% of annual sales + inventory
Gas Stations (w/o C-Store)	15–20% of annual sales + inventory
Gift/Card Shops	35% of annual sales incl. inventory
Grocery Store (Supermarket)	15% of annuals sales + inventory
Hardware Stores	45% of annual sales incl. inventory

Industry	Rule of Thumb Valuation
Insurance Agencies	125–150% of annual revenues
Landscape Businesses	45% of annual sales
Law Practices	90–100% of annuals revenues
Liquor Stores	40–45% of annuals sales + inventory
Restaurants (Full-Serve)	30–35% of annuals sales + inventory
Restaurants (Ltd-Serve)	30–40% of annuals sales + inventory
Sporting Goods Stores	25% of annual sales + inventory
Taverns/Bars	40% of annuals sales + inventory
Travel Agencies	35–40% of annual commissions
Veterinary Practices	70% of annual revenues + inventory

Does the Rule of Thumb Appraisal Method apply to your business or to your acquisition target?

EBITDA Appraisal Method

EBITDA is an acronym for E̲arnings B̲efore I̲nterest, T̲axes, D̲epreciation, and A̲mortization. The EBITDA Appraisal Method attempts to remove all the factors that are viable from one owner to the next in privately held businesses. That said, the EBITDA Appraisal Method is most often use for public companies where their enterprise value can be computed.

In privately held businesses, one owner may have to borrow money while the next may pay in cash. Therefore, interest on debt is removed as a consideration. Likewise, since taxes for any business other than a C-corp can vary based on the owner's tax bracket, taxes are removed to determine a common earning capacity. Since new depreciation and amortization values will be established after the sale, they too are removed.

The EBITDA Appraisal Method is often used to appraise the value of larger businesses than those appraised with the Rule of Thumb Appraisal Method. However, similar to the Rule of Thumb Appraisal Method, the resulting earnings are calculated using the EBITDA Appraisal Method and then multiplied by some value based on comparable companies in that industry based on their earnings numbers.

The EBITDA Appraisal Method is used for many industrial

and consumer industries, but not for banks, insurance, oil & gas, or real estate businesses. These industries do not use the EBITDA Appraisal Method because they have extenuating circumstances that affect their value. For these industries, the range of the earnings multiple is adjusted based on the business's market dominance, lack of stock liquidity if they are private, any long-term debt, and of course risk. Generally, the bigger the company, the less risk there is and the higher a multiple they can command.

When it comes to public companies, you can often see valuations of 20-30 times EBITDA. However, this is generally not the case in privately held companies. One of the reasons for the higher multiple of public companies is size and liquidity. Since the stockholders of public companies can easily buy or sell their stocks, they have more liquidity. In comparison, the buying and selling of stocks is not very easily done with private companies.

The following table is an estimate of the EBITDA multiple by industry and size.

Industry	EBITDA			
	$1 Million	$5 Million	$10 Million	$25 Million
Service	4.0	5.0	6.0	6.0
Manufacturing	4.0	5.3	6.0	6.0
Retail	2.5	5.0	5.8	No Data
Distribution	3.0	4.0	5.0	5.5
Restaurant	2.5	5.0	5.3	No Data
Healthcare	5.0	5.0	7.0	7.5
Technology	5.5	6.5	6.5	7.5

Does the EBITDA Appraisal Method apply to your business or to your acquisition target?

Discounted Cash Flow Appraisal Method

The Discounted Cash Flow Appraisal Method is also used for larger businesses similar to the EBITDA method.

To understand the Discounted Cash Flow Appraisal Method, one needs to understand the concept of the "time value of money." If you invest a dollar and it earns you a 10% annual return, that dollar would be worth $1.10 in one year. Therefore, if I agree to give you a dollar in one year, it is not actually worth the same as if I gave you a dollar today. Since you aren't able to invest it and let it grow over time, you would only have $1.00 next year instead of $1.10. To determine what a dollar in the future is worth today, I have to discount the future value to get to the present value. Therefore $.91 today invested at 10% will be worth $1.00 in one year ($.91 + $.09 interest = $1.00).

This principle is the basis for the Discounted Cash Flow Appraisal Method. Generally, the Discounted Cash Flow Appraisal Method attempts to use past performance to project the free cash flow in the future. Generally, sellers and buyers agree on projected future earnings 5 years into the future. Then a discount is applied to the future cash flows in years 2-5 to determine their net present value. By adding up the net present values of future earnings, a valuation is determined. Of course the discount applied to the future cash flows is a subjective number and is broadly based on risk factors.

Does the Discounted Cash Flow Appraisal Method apply to your business or to your acquisition target?

Comparable Company/Transaction Appraisal Method

Companies like Business Valuation Resources and Bizcomps are leading providers of information about private company transactions. They sell reports to business brokers, which they can use to do comparable company searches and evaluations. When it comes to valuations using comparable companies, the values are based on a lot of financial analysis data such as net sales, cash flow, net income, book value, gross profit, etc.

Inc. magazine used to publish this data every few years or so. However, they have not published this data since 2009. The data from the 2009 issue of Inc. is impossible to locate on the internet, but I saved a copy years ago as a reference for my clients. You can find it under the Resource tab of SteveBizBlog.com.

Not only does this reference provide comparable company valuations, it also looks at which appraisal methods are the most accurate and ways to predict their value based on industry type. While the data is a bit dated, it is free and should give you a rough idea of a company's worth.

Based upon comparable transaction data, what is your business or target acquisition worth?

Asset Accumulation Appraisal Method

The Asset Accumulation Appraisal Method is used primarily for real estate holding companies, oil & gas companies, or other asset heavy companies with earnings that do not support a value higher than the tangible assets. This method is sometimes used with profitable companies to represent the low end of the range of indications of value. This method also sets the bar that valuation methods based on earnings must overcome to show proof of goodwill value.

The Asset Accumulation Appraisal Method is the process for computing the market value of a business's tangible and intangible assets and liabilities. This process starts with the sum of all tangible assets as reflected on the company balance sheet. A discount or step up is then applied to ascertain what it would cost to obtain comparable assets in similar condition today. To determine the market value of comparable tangible assets, you can contact used equipment dealers and/or auctioneers.

From there, the sum of the business's tangible liabilities are deducted from the adjusted asset value. Then to the working value you would add of any off balance sheet or intangible assets, or in other words, the assets that wouldn't normally appear on the balance sheet.

Off Balance Sheet/Intangible assets include:

- Trade/Service Marks
- Customer List
- Staff/Employees
- Licensing, Royalty, or Other Standing Agreements
- Use rights (e.g., drilling, water, or mineral)
- Service Contracts
- Trade Secrets
- Patented Technologies

Finally, you deduct a value for any contingent liabilities such as pending legal action judgments and costs associated with regulatory compliance to come up with the final valuation.

Using the Asset Accumulation Appraisal Method, what is your business or target acquisition worth?

Liquidation Appraisal Method

When it comes to non-profitable businesses, the Liquidation Appraisal Method is used. For this method, only the value of the tangible assets is used. The reason behind this is the buyer is only purchasing the tangible assets. Any liabilities of the business entity are the responsibility of the seller and are not factored into the appraisal valuation since the buyer is not buying the business, but just the tangible assets.

When the value of the assets are calculated using the Liquidation Appraisal Method, it is assumed that they are being sold in an orderly selloff and not under any duress in the form of a fire sale.

Using the Liquidation Appraisal Method, what is your business or target acquisition worth?

Chapter 3: The Deal

Process Mistakes that Reduce a Business's Value During a Sale

Between the time when a business owner puts his company on the market and the closing date, there are two events that can occur which either kill the deal outright or negatively affect the final sale – the inadvertent disclosure of the sale and the accidental disclosure of proprietary information to competitors and customers.

The most common is the inadvertent disclosure of the impending sale. When the sale is unexpected and word leaks out in an uncontrolled manner, it has the very real potential to sink the deal in a variety of ways. For one, when employees discover that the company is for sale, they wonder what else they don't know and become concerned that they may be on a sinking ship. They may put out feelers and begin to look at other employment options. As key employees leave, the value of the business is negatively affected. The entire sale may die if enough people leave. Moreover, employees that feel blindsided may lose respect for the company and management, affecting their performance even if they stay.

The inadvertent disclosure of the sale may also cause customers to question the reason why the owner is selling. They may begin to look for alternatives, fearing that unwelcome changes may occur after the sale. Competitors can use the news of the sale to pirate your best customers and employees. Even your suppliers may start selling to your competitors because they are uneasy about the future.

Go to this book's video supplement page at www.stevebizblog.com/buysell-videos to see a video of John Zayac, the owner of IBG a large M&A brokerage house, explaining how an inadvertent disclosure can submarine a deal.

In addition to the inadvertent disclosure of the sale and all the negative things that snowball out of it, sometimes during the due diligence process the seller will discloses proprietary information to competitors and customers. Generally, the potential buyer is covered by a confidentiality agreement. However, the due diligence process performed by the buyer sometimes creates enough confusion that proprietary information is mistakenly disclosed. Someone somewhere makes the incorrect assumption that what they are discussing isn't consider proprietary and word leaks out. Once the bullet has left the gun, there is no getting it back.

How will you protect against inadvertent disclosures?

So, You Decided To Sell – The Documentation

Whether you are using a business broker or attempting to sell your business yourself, you will need to start with a solid business plan. Using the business plan as your base, you will need to edit it to create a confidential business review document (CBR). The CBR is the main document buyers will use to evaluate your business.

One primary area where the CBR document differs from a standard business plan is in finances. Generally, you will want to include a 3 year look at past P&L performance. You will then want to take your 12 month trailing P&L and recast it to show it in a more favorable and objective light. Next, you will want to develop a 5 year proforma to show the potential buyer what he might expect in the coming years. A word of caution – If you paint too rosy a picture, the potential buyer may use it to his advantage and tie your exaggerated projections to an earn-out. Finally, you'll want to prepare a complete list of all the furniture, fixtures, and other tangible assets with their market price.

When it comes to the marketing plan, you will want to add any independent research about your industry to educate potential buyers who many not be very familiar with your industry. When it comes to the operational plan, you may want to include bios and images of the key members of your business.

As an appendix to the CBR document, you will want to include pictures of your office, key assets, and other images that will give the potential buyer a better idea of your business.

Once the CBR document is complete, you will want to create a one page executive summary that you will use as a flier. You will want the executive summary to include key financial and other information that will attract a potential buyer. However, your executive summary should not disclose enough about the business that anyone can track it back to your company. You need to be vague enough to avoid inadvertent disclosure yet convey enough tantalizing information to make the potential buyer want to sign a non disclosure agreement (NDA) to get your CBR document. Therefore, in the scheme of things, you make the executive summary a publicly available document and use the NDA as a gate to your CBR document.

Once your marketing materials are produced, it is a good idea to make copies of all contracts, agreements, financial records, corporate governance documents, tax returns, policies, etc. and assemble a due diligence box.

Have you prepared the documents required to make a buyer feel like he has all the facts to make a decision?

What to Expect During Due Diligence

When I sold my first company, I got a call from my business broker just before I was packing up to go home one night. He said that there was some interest in my business by a potential out-of-state buyer. He added they were a publicly traded company and wanted to fly out a team to conduct their due diligence on my business and make the offer in person. They wanted to see if my business was a good fit for them. When I asked my broker when were they planning to come, he said they wanted to come out the day after tomorrow because time was of the essence.

Had I not had a pretty comprehensive collection of due diligence materials beforehand, I would have been in panic mode. I had made copies of every contract, agreement, and three years of historical financial records. I also had copies of my minute books and other corporate governance documents. Finally, I had copies for 3 years of tax returns as well as policies, procedures, and personnel records. The list of documents was pretty extensive and nearly filled a copy paper box.

I learned later that the due diligence team was very impressed with the completeness of our preparation. Had I not had assembled all the information they were looking for, they would not have been able to complete the due diligence to meet their timetable and likely would have passed on the deal. As it was, my due diligence planning was a major factor in selling my first business.

The due diligence team consisted of their CEO, CFO, Corporate Lawyer, Marketing and Sales VP, and Human Resources Representative.

The CEO's role was to determine if we were a strategic fit and if our acquisition worked with his vision. T

he CFO examined our finances. He sat down with our bookkeeper and CPA and performed a series of financial analysis to determine how our ratios compared with others in our industry.

Then there was their corporate lawyer who reviewed all our contacts and agreements to look for potential liabilities.

Next was their Marketing and Sales VP who grilled my team to determine our market potential.

Finally, there was a representative from Human Resources who examined our employment and payroll records and spoke to some of our key employees.

When I sold another business, it was to a single high-net buyer. That sale was quite different as he performed much of the due diligence himself. That said, he took copies of a few documents and asked if he could share them with some of his advisers, including his CPA and lawyer. Here again, we presented the buyer with a complete collection of records, which certainly went a long way in convincing the buyer we had nothing to hide.

Your job as the seller is to establish premium value for your business and close the credibility gap. Being prepared for the onslaught that is the due diligence analysis goes a long way to establish value and credibility. I have an extensive list of due diligence items that we used when I was part of a public company and we needed to look at acquisition targets. This list is available under "Resources" on SteveBizBlog.com. While the list is over the top for most due diligence process, it's an exhaustive list of the items that may affect the buyer.

Are you prepared for a due diligence inspection of your business?

Forms of M&A Payments

Most buyers and sellers just assume that when you buy or sell a business you pay **cash**. While cash may be a component in the sales price, generally a business sale is never an all cash deal. Often, there are secured and/or unsecured notes that the seller my extend to the buyer. Of course, a secured note will cost the buyer more than an unsecured note. If the buyer is a corporation, some or all of the purchase price may be in the form of stock. Of course, stock in a private company is quiet different from stock in a public company, especially from a liquidity standpoint.

If you receive **stock** as part of the purchase price, you must determine if the shares are restricted or unrestricted. If the buyer issues restricted shares, it means that the seller cannot cash out immediately after the sale and dump large quantities of stock that can adversely affected the buyers stock price. Moreover, there are many tax issues and options with restricted shares. It is highly recommended that sellers seek financial and tax advise when sale price includes stock.

Another form of payment is known as an **earn-out**. An earn-out is where the seller gets paid based on the post-sale performance of the business.

After the sale, the buyer often does not want the seller to start a competing business. After all, the seller could easily steal back his previous employees, customers and vendors.

To address this problem, the buyer often allocates some of the sale price to a **non-compete agreement**.

Sometimes the buyer wants the seller to remain partially or fully engaged with the business. In this case, the buyer may offer a **consulting or employment agreement** to the seller.

Also, the seller may agree to a **royalty or licensing agreement** with the seller as part of the overall deal.

As you can see, there are many options that a buyer can use other than cash on the barrel head to compensate the seller.

Go to this book's video supplement page at www.stevebizblog.com/buysell-videos to see a video of Tom James, a lawyer who's practice specializes in M&A, explaining forms of payment he often sees with his clients.

What forms of payment are you willing to accept during the sale of your business?

Allocation of Sales Price Governs Tax Consequences

Once you agree on a final price for the business, the seller and buyer must agree to what portion of the purchase price applies to the tangible assets vs. intangible assets (e.g., goodwill).

The allocation of the purchase price will dictate what portion of the sale price the seller can treat as capital gains vs. ordinary income tax. In turn, this could dramatically affect the net proceeds of the seller and future tax treatment for the buyer. As Robert Kiyosaki once said, "It is not how much money you make, but how much you get to keep." When it comes to selling a business, this statement could not be more true.

What is good for the seller's tax picture is often bad for the buyer and vice versa. Therefore, the allocation of price to various components of the deal is frequently an area for negotiation and compromise.

The difference between your tax basis and your proceeds from the sale is what is taxable. The seller's tax basis is generally the original cost of the asset, minus the accumulated depreciation deductions claimed, minus any casualty losses claimed, plus any additional paid-in capital and selling expenses. The seller's proceeds from the sale generally include the total sales price, plus any additional liabilities the buyer takes over from the seller, if any. For example, a transferable liability could be long term debt in a stock purchase.

As the seller, you will probably want to allocate most, if not all, of the purchase price to the capital assets that were transferred with the business. The seller wants to do that because proceeds from the sale of a capital asset, including business property, are taxed as long term capital gains, which is lower than ordinary income. Long term capital gains are taxed for most people at 15% for everyone except the super wealthy while ordinary income is taxed at between 10% and 39.6% based on your marginal income tax rate.

After the sale, the buyer will be able to depreciate or amortize most of the assets that were transferred. Because different types of assets are depreciated differently under IRS rules, the buyer will want to allocate more of the price toward assets that can be depreciated quickly and less of the price to ones that must be depreciated over 15 years or longer (e.g., goodwill, buildings, and land).

Since most transactions are treated as an asset sale, allocating the sales price between the various assets is a serious negotiation between the buyer and seller. The buyer wants as much money as possible to be allocated to items that are currently deductible, such as a consulting agreement or assets that can be depreciated quickly. This will improve the business's cash flow and reduce its tax bill.

The seller, however, wants as much money as possible allocated to assets on which the gain is treated as a capital gain rather than assets on which gain must be treated as ordinary income. Given that most small business owners who are successful in selling their company are in a high tax bracket, this rate differential is very important in reducing tax liability.

Go to this book's video supplement page at www.stevebizblog.com/buysell-videos to see a video of Chris Blees, the President and CEO of a large CPA firm specializing in M&A transactions, explaining how structuring the payment of a business sale can effect the sellers and buyers taxes post sale.

It is always a good idea to get tax advice from a CPA with experience in mergers and acquisition when structuring a deal either as the seller or buyer.

How much thought have you given to the allocation of the sales price?

He Who Mentions Price First Loses

When it comes to buying a business, buyers buy a documented and believable future. If you are the seller, it is your job to explain the past and sell the future. While it is up to the seller to prove the value of the business, it is often not a good idea for the seller to volunteer a price. As the old saying goes, "He who mentions price first loses." Once a price is mentioned by the seller, there is really no chance that the price will ever go higher and it becomes a cap.

It is worth noting that the buyer may be a strategic buyer and may not be buying what you think you are selling. In fact, D. Peter Drucker put it succinctly when he said,

"The buyer rarely buys what the seller thinks he's selling."

Generally, it is up to the buyer to define the price after reviewing the seller's business.

Go to this book's video supplement page at www.stevebizblog.com/buysell-videos to see a video of Ron Chernak and John Zayac two owners of M&A brokerage houses, explaining when you should list a price for a business and when to leave it up to the buyer to define the price.

Do you explain the past and sell the future without

mentioning price?

Value of Due Diligence

The other day I had a client look at buying someone's business. The seller was very anxious to close the deal quickly which was the first indication that there might be a problem.

Looking at the finances for the prior three years, revenue and profits were definitely moving in the right direction and the buyer was eager to ink the deal, fearing that someone else would beat them to the punch. I urged the client to complete his due diligence before committing to the deal. Fortunately, the client took my advise.

In the subsequent due diligence, he discovered that the seller had a very low reorder rate, signaling that the seller's product was not that well received. Further, we discovered that the seller was experiencing high employee turn over, perhaps indicating they didn't pay enough for the work they expected from their employees. Finally, we noticed that their customer acquisition costs were rising and their gross margins were shrinking.

While I often tell clients looking at buying someone else's business that the deal has to make sense financially, you also have to make sure you complete your due diligence and analyze all aspects of the business.

Do you do your due diligence before you make a purchase?

How to Argue for Seller Financing

Most banks say that they are small business lenders. The missing part of that statement is how banks define small businesses and what banks will lend money for.

From the bank's prospective, a small business is an established business and not a new business. Moreover, banks lend money primarily for tangible assets that double as collateral. Banks rarely lend money to start up a business since there is not a track record of success and when they do, they only lend money for tangible assets.

For the most part, banks are very conservative in their lending practices to businesses so they can stay within the rules to maintain their required FDIC insurance. Therefore, when you consider that the average main street business has minimal tangible assets and sells for $350k and the average buyer has less the $100k in cash, where does the other $250k come from if not from the bank? The answer is the seller of course.

While the seller would prefer that the buyer secure the full purchase price from other sources, he will often have no other choice but to be the lender to the buyer. Let's face it, a bank's only recourse if the borrower defaults on the loan is to sell off the assets of the business, which are often very specialized and not very liquid, for a steep discount. However, the seller could step in and take over the business again since he is familiar with the operations, inventory, equipment, employees, and customers, and perhaps even sell it again.

Most banks work with the SBA to help fund business loans and generally involve either real estate or other tangible, yet relatively liquid assets, such as a fleet vehicle. Moreover, only about 20% of all deals are financed at least in part with an SBA loan. This leaves a rather large gap between the business's sale price and what the buyer can fund personally or through some form of bank financing if he wants to sell.

Furthermore, the seller knows the real cash flow of the business to the buyer while lenders can only rely on what is reported on the books and the business's tax returns.

Additionally, if the seller is willing to carry back part of the note, the buyer feels more assured that the seller is not hiding something. This bridges the leap of faith gap that the buyer has to make. Moreover, since the seller has some skin in the game, the buyer has an adviser for the term of the loan since the seller has capital at risk if the buyer does not succeed.

As a rule of thumb, the buyer puts down 20% to 50% at closing and has the seller or a third party finances the rest.

A typical scenario is one third down, one third financed by a third party like a bank for the liquid tangible assets, and one third carried by the seller.

Remember that in addition to the money put down at closing, the buyer will need cash for working capital since the seller normally pockets the cash and all accounts receivable earned under his watch.

A down payment rule of thumb is that the down payment should equal about one year's discretionary earnings after accounting for debt service. For example, if you put down $50k, you should have $50k in discretionary income after you subtract your annual debt on the loan.

Have you ever considered buyer financing when buying someone else's business?

Seller Financed Earn Out

Another way to get the seller to finance a portion of the sale price is to use what is known as an earn out. Earn outs are most commonly used when it is less clear whether or not the seller is truly representing the value of the company's future earning potential. In an earn out, the buyer's down payment covers at a minimum the purchase of all the business assets. Then, a schedule is defined that plots various earnings and correlates them to future payments to the seller.

Let's say you agree to pay the seller $350k for his business and the valuation is basing on being able to exceed one million dollars in revenue each year. However, the buyer is skeptical that a million dollars in revenue is a real possibility. In this case, the buyer would use an earn out tied to the sellers projected millions dollars in sales.

To be more specific, the buyer might agree to pay the seller at closing $100k to cover the purchase of the business assets and further agree that if the business exceeds the projected one million dollar in sales for the next two years, the buyer will pay the seller an additional $125k in each of the next two years, adding up the remaining $250k.

However, if the business does between $999 and $900k (less than the target revenue), the buyer would agree to pay only $75k instead of the $125K. If the business does less than $800k, he will make no payment that year at all.

Likewise, in an earn out, if the projected target was say one million and the business did 1.5 million, there would an upside built in for the seller and he may receive perhaps $200k for those years.

In the end, an earn out is an effective way to hedge your bets if you are not sure how the business will perform after the sale or if you think the seller is over selling his business.

Have you ever considered an earn out when buying someone else's business?

www.ingramcontent.com/pod-product-compliance
Lightning Source LLC
Chambersburg PA
CBHW071823200526

45169CB00018B/925